HOME
for the
Holidays

A HAND-CRAFTED COLORING BOOK

Illustrations by Galadriel A.L. Thompson

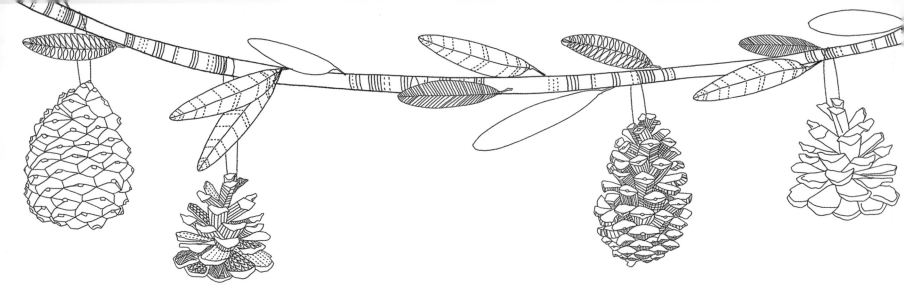

Published in 2016 by: Spirit Marketing, LLC
700 Broadway Boulevard, Suite 101, Kansas City, MO 64105

hellospiritmarketing.com
© 2016 Spirit Marketing

ISBN: 978-0-9965998-0-1

Designed in Kansas City by
Chris Evans, Galadriel A. L. Thompson, Chris Simmons,
and Patrick Sullivan.

For information about custom editions, special sales, and premium and corporate purchases, please contact Spirit Marketing at info@hellospiritmail.com or 1.888.288.3972.

Printed 6/16 - 7/16 in China

This book belongs to:

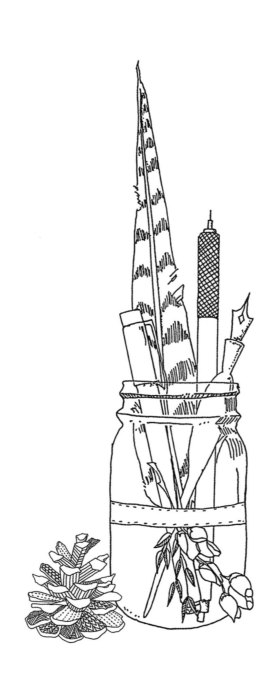

Galadriel A. L. Thompson

A visual artist with vast creative and technical experience, Galadriel thrives on bringing art to life through intricate, hand-drawn designs. Focusing on the beauty that surrounds us, and can sometimes go unnoticed, Galadriel centers on highlighting that beauty for all to experience in new, intriguing ways.

Born in Tulsa, she has since moved to Kansas City with her wild tribe of three children and holds a BFA in animation from the Kansas City Art Institute. She works as a freelance illustrator and animator creating album cover art, promotional pieces and music videos for bands across the Midwest and Pacific Northwest. Galadriel is also a co-founder of MusicKC, an organization that helps build the arts infrastructure for Kansas City's music community.

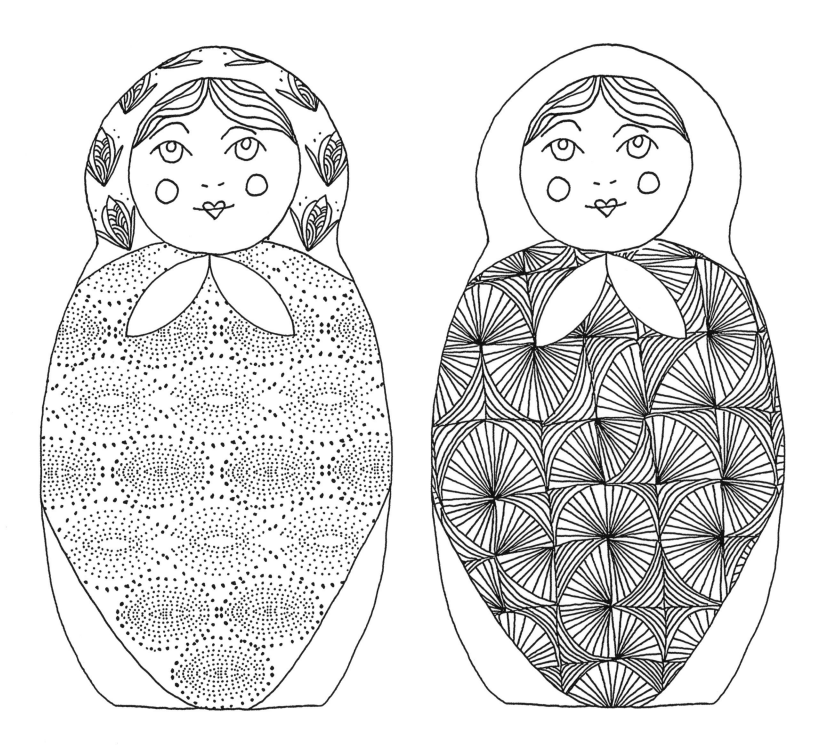

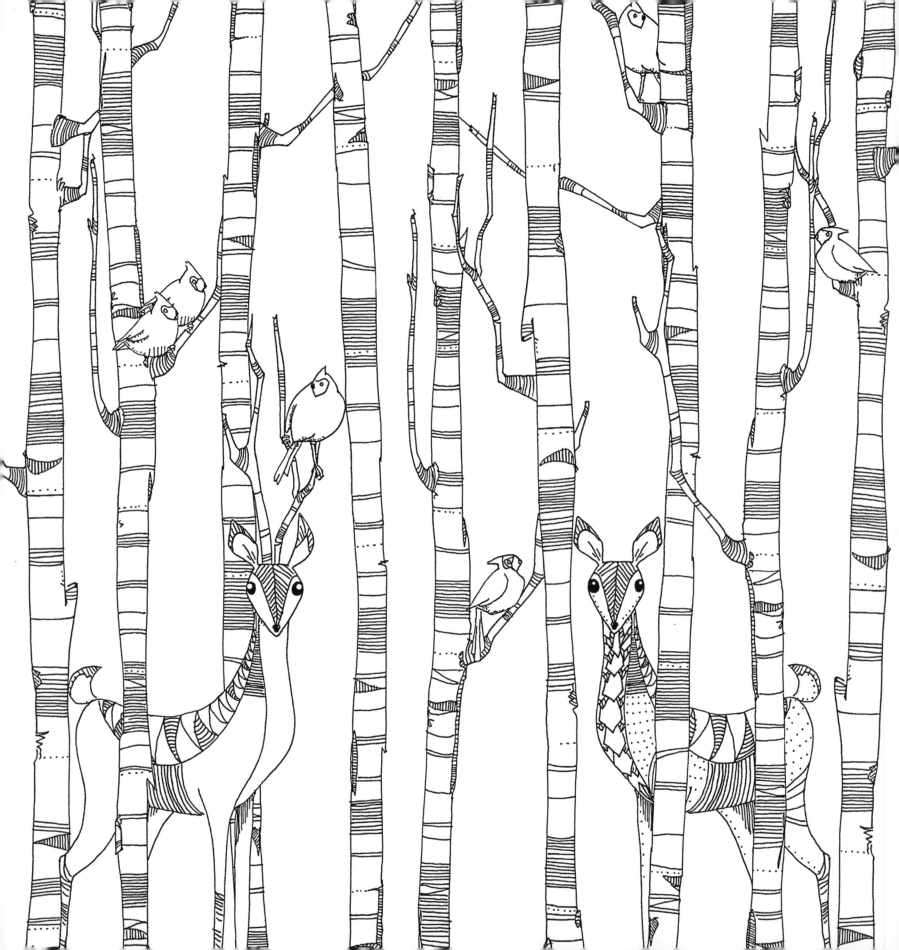